W9-AKT-687

SCHOOL SHOOTINGS

by Jen Barton

BrightP◆int Press

San Diego, CA

BrightPoint Press

© 2020 BrightPoint Press
an imprint of ReferencePoint Press, Inc.
Printed in the United States

For more information, contact:
BrightPoint Press
PO Box 27779
San Diego, CA 92198
www.BrightPointPress.com

LIBRARY OF CONGRESS CATALOGING-IN-PUBLICATION DATA

Names: Barton, Jen, author.
Title: School shootings / Jen Barton.
Description: San Diego, CA : ReferencePoint Press, Inc., [2020] | Series: In
   focus | Audience: Grade 9 to 12. | Includes bibliographical references and
   index.
Identifiers: LCCN 2019003312 (print) | LCCN 2019011227 (ebook) | ISBN
   9781682827222 (ebook) | ISBN 9781682827215 (hardcover)
Subjects: LCSH: School shootings--United States--Juvenile literature. |
   School shootings--Prevention--Juvenile literature.
Classification: LCC LB3013.32 (ebook) | LCC LB3013.32 .B37 2020 (print) | DDC
   371.7/82--dc23
LC record available at https://lccn.loc.gov/2019003312

CONTENTS

TIMELINE

April 16, 2007
A shooter kills thirty-two people at Virginia Polytechnic Institute in Virginia. He injures seventeen others. He later kills himself.

September 1994
The Federal Assault Weapons Ban becomes law. The ban makes it illegal to manufacture and own certain semiautomatic weapons for noncombat use.

September 2004
The Federal Assault Weapons Ban expires. Lawmakers try to renew it but are unsuccessful.

1990 **2000** **2002** **2004** **2006**

April 20, 1999
Two shooters kill thirteen people at Columbine High School in Colorado. They injure twenty-one people. The shooters also kill themselves.

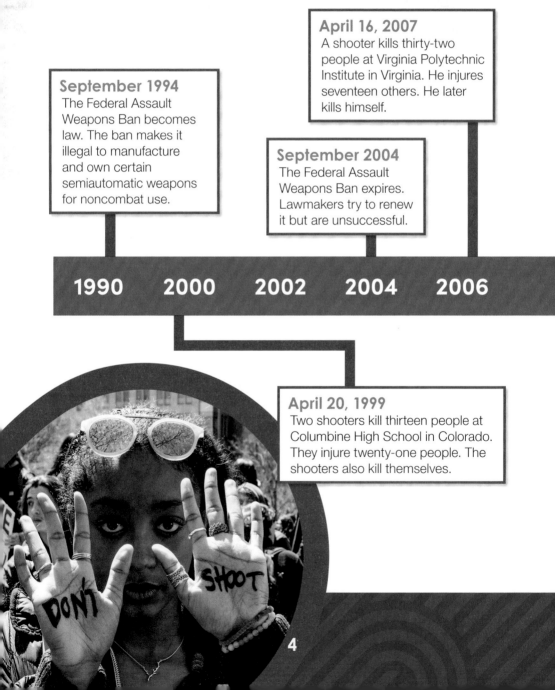

March 24, 2018
Shooting survivors lead the March for Our Lives protest.

2008   2010   2012   2014   2018

December 14, 2012
A shooter kills twenty-six people at Sandy Hook Elementary School in Connecticut. He injures two others. He later kills himself.

June 26, 2008
The US Supreme Court decides a case called *District of Columbia v. Heller*. It rules that people have the right to own and use guns for self-defense.

February 14, 2018
A shooter kills seventeen people at Marjory Stoneman Douglas High School in Florida. He injures seventeen others.

SHOTS RING OUT

Fourteen-year-old Eden Hebron was in school on February 14, 2018. She attended Marjory Stoneman Douglas High School in Parkland, Florida. She heard shots ring out. She was in the middle of a writing exam. At first, she was not scared. She thought it was a prank. But the shots continued. Eden and her classmates hid under a table, terrified. Her friend was

More than 3,000 students attend Marjory Stoneman Douglas High School.

beside her. They heard the shots coming

closer. Then the gunman was right outside

their classroom. Eden heard glass from

the door shatter. The gunman shot into

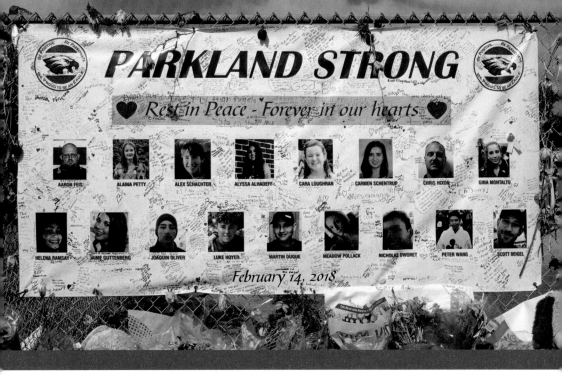

The Parkland community created a memorial for the school shooting victims.

the room. Eden thought she would not

make it out alive. Bullets hit her friend. Eden

watched her friend die. She wondered if she

would be next.

Eden survived the shooting. But she

struggled emotionally. She grieved for her

friend and the sixteen others who had

been killed. Fourteen of the victims were students. Three were staff members. It was the deadliest high school shooting in US history.

DEFINING SCHOOL SHOOTINGS

Some sources say 2018 was the worst year on record for school shootings. The Naval Postgraduate School (NPS) began to collect school shootings data in 1970. It documented ninety-four school shootings in 2018. This was far more than any other year.

There is no standard definition for *school shooting*. Many sources disagree on the definition. The NPS counts any time a person shows a gun on school property. Even if the gun is not fired, the NPS counts it as a shooting. Other sources have narrower definitions. *Education Week* is a news organization. It also collected data about school shootings in 2018. It documented twenty-four school shootings. It counts every time a gun is fired on school property. It also counts every time a gun is fired on a school bus. It does not count **suicides** or self-inflicted injuries.

Despite the confusion over this definition, most people agree that school shootings

Students raise awareness of school shootings at a protest in Washington, DC, in 2018.

are a problem. Many groups are trying

to address the issue. Activists organize

protest marches to raise awareness.

Politicians propose laws to strengthen gun control. Researchers study gun violence to gather information. They hope their studies will help people better understand the issue. But with an issue this complicated, there is no easy answer.

Activists of all ages are involved in the fight against gun violence.

CHAPTER ONE

WHAT IS THE HISTORY OF SCHOOL SHOOTINGS?

School shootings have been happening for a long time. One of the first school shootings in the United States happened in 1840. A student shot a professor at the University of Virginia. The professor died three days later. Still, the rate of gun

Newspaper headlines report a school shooting at Santa Fe High School in Texas in 2018.

violence in schools was low in the 1800s

and early 1900s.

Gun violence in schools increased in the

1970s. One of the worst school shootings

during this time happened in Fullerton,

California. A custodian brought a gun to California State University on June 12, 1976. He opened fire in the school's library. He killed seven people. He injured two others.

THE BATH SCHOOL BOMBING

The deadliest school disaster in US history occurred in 1927. Andrew Kehoe planted explosives underneath a school. The school was in Bath Township, Michigan. Kehoe was a member of the school board. The bomb went off on the morning of May 18. It killed thirty-six children and two teachers. Kehoe later drove to the school. His truck was loaded with more explosives. When he arrived at the school, he fired into his truck. The truck blew up. Kehoe and four other people were killed.

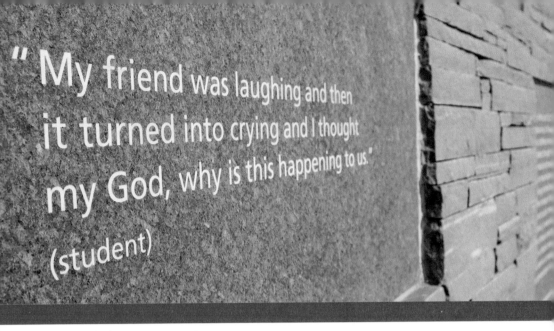

"My friend was laughing and then it turned into crying and I thought my God, why is this happening to us."

(student)

A memorial in Littleton, Colorado, shares people's memories of the 1999 Columbine High School shooting.

The rate of school shootings spiked again in the early 1990s. School shootings with multiple victims became more common. In some cases, these may be called mass shootings. There is no legal definition of *mass shooting*. The US government's definition is a shooting with at least four victims.

One of the deadliest school shootings in US history happened on April 20, 1999. Two shooters came into Columbine High School. This school is in Littleton, Colorado. The shooters were students at the school. They killed thirteen people. They also killed themselves. They injured twenty-one others.

SCHOOL SHOOTINGS TODAY

Studies show that school shootings have become more common in recent years. The Parkland incident was the deadliest US school shooting in 2018. Another school shooting happened three months later. It occurred on May 18 at Santa Fe

Memorial crosses on the grounds of Santa Fe High School remember the ten people killed in the shooting.

High School. This school is in Santa Fe, Texas. A student took two guns into school. He opened fire in a classroom. He killed ten people. Eight of the victims were students.

Two were teachers. The shooter wounded thirteen others.

RESEARCHING SCHOOL SHOOTINGS

Many researchers study school shootings. Studies show that school shootings are rare. Few students experience them. Some researchers even believe school shootings are decreasing. James Alan Fox is a professor of criminology at Northeastern University. He studied school shootings in 2018. He collected data from many sources. He found that there were more shootings involving students in the 1990s than there are today. He also found that since then,

LOCKDOWN DRILLS

Lockdown drills prepare students and teachers for a threat. A threat occurs when a dangerous person is near or inside the school. In these cases, schools follow a lockdown procedure. Drills help them practice this procedure. Students and teachers stay in classrooms during a lockdown drill. They clear out of the hallways. Everyone must be quiet. Teachers turn off classroom lights. They lock all doors and windows. These actions may help keep people safe during a shooting.

this number has been decreasing. Fox says, "Schools are safer today than they had been in previous decades."[1]

Fox's findings differ from many other studies. Other studies show that school shootings are increasing. This difference may be because there is no

standard definition of school shootings.

Researchers' definitions may differ.

Because of this, some facts about school

EVERYTOWN FOR GUN SAFETY

Everytown for Gun Safety is a gun control group. It published a map in 2014. The map tracked US school shootings that had happened since a 2012 mass shooting. This shooting had occurred at Sandy Hook Elementary School in Connecticut. Everytown said that seventy-four school shootings had happened since then. Some experts disagreed with these results. Everytown counted unintentional shootings. It also counted shootings that had happened near schools. Some people thought this definition was too broad.

shootings remain unclear. Agreeing on definitions is important. This could help researchers and others better understand school shootings.

The media has helped more people become aware of school shootings. Mass shootings are widely broadcast on the news. Social media also helps spread the word. But shootings with one or a few victims usually receive less attention.

GUN VIOLENCE

School shootings are part of the larger issue of gun violence. Experts agree that students are at risk. The threat comes from weapons and violence in general. Garen Wintemute

is an emergency room doctor. He is also

a researcher at the University of California,

Davis. He studies gun violence. He says,

"The best way to prevent school shootings

is to prevent shootings in general."[2]

The Centers for Disease Control and

Prevention (CDC) published a study in

2015. The CDC collected data on violence

and deaths in US schools. The data

came from students of all ages. They

ranged in age from five to eighteen. The

CDC looked at data from 1992 to 2015.

It found that murder was the second main

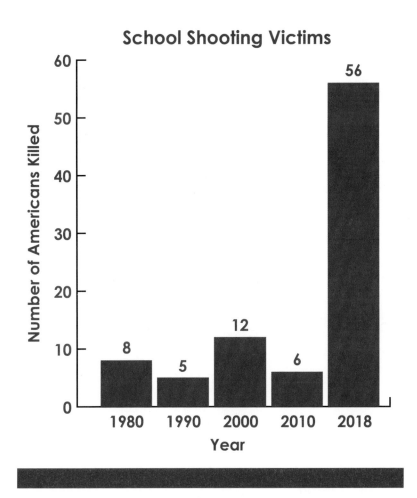

School Shooting Victims

Number of Americans Killed (y-axis: 0, 10, 20, 30, 40, 50, 60)

Year (x-axis): 1980, 1990, 2000, 2010, 2018

- 1980: 8
- 1990: 5
- 2000: 12
- 2010: 6
- 2018: 56

This graph shows the number of Americans killed in school shootings in certain years from 1980 to 2018. The data comes from the Naval Postgraduate School.

cause of death for kids in this age group.

Other researchers study different racial

groups. Some study African American

Activists play dead to protest gun violence in Washington, DC, in 2018. This type of protest is called a lie-in.

children and teens. Gun violence is the

number one cause of death among

this group.

Studies show that just being around

violence can be damaging. Some people

are exposed to violence at a young age. This can cause long-term harm. The effects can last into adulthood. People who have witnessed violence have high rates of depression. They often have a lot of anxiety. This can lead to drug and alcohol abuse. It can even cause post-traumatic stress disorder (PTSD). PTSD is a mental health condition. People who go through life-threatening events often have PTSD. They have trouble sleeping. They relive the event over and over again. They may feel afraid even when they are not in danger.

CHAPTER TWO

HOW ARE PEOPLE ADDRESSING SCHOOL SHOOTINGS?

Passing laws is one way to address
school shootings. In 1994, President
Bill Clinton signed a gun control **bill**.
The law was called the Federal Assault
Weapons Ban (AWB). The AWB banned

Many activists are fighting to reinstate the ban on assault weapons.

the manufacture and ownership of certain

semiautomatic guns. These guns eject and

load ammunition automatically. This allows

many shots to be fired quickly. The guns

were designed for combat. The AWB said

Today, Bill Clinton gives speeches across the country. He continues to support gun control.

they should not be available to the public.

Law enforcement was exempt from the

ban. So was the military.

The AWB was passed in response to two mass shootings. One was a school shooting. It happened on January 17, 1989. A shooter entered Cleveland Elementary School in Stockton, California. He killed five children. He wounded twenty-nine others. He also killed himself. He used a semiautomatic gun. This was the deadliest school shooting in the 1980s. In 1991, a shooter entered a restaurant in Killeen, Texas. He was armed with two semiautomatic guns. He killed twenty-two people. He injured twenty others.

RISING GUN VIOLENCE

Mass shootings decreased after the AWB was passed. The ban expired in 2004. Some lawmakers tried to renew it. But they were unsuccessful. Mass shootings increased after the AWB expired. Experts are unsure whether this was a direct result of the ban ending. There may have been other causes. Some experts think media coverage played a role. Media coverage can encourage copycat shooters. Copycat shooters commit violence after seeing examples of it in the media. This might help explain the rise in mass shootings in

Senator Dianne Feinstein has represented California in Congress since 1992.

the early 2000s. Media coverage of gun

violence increased at this time.

California senator Dianne Feinstein

supports the AWB. Feinstein and two

other senators introduced a bill in 2019.

It is called the Assault Weapons Ban of 2019. It proposes to ban military-style assault weapons. Feinstein said, "We need to get these weapons of war off our streets."[3]

THE SECOND AMENDMENT

People use the Second **Amendment** to argue for gun ownership rights. This amendment is one sentence long. It guarantees "the right of the people to keep and bear arms."[4] The amendment's language is not very clear. Many courts have interpreted it. They have said the right does not apply to all people. People

THIS IS OUR LANE

The American College of Physicians published a paper in 2018. It called gun violence a public health threat. It recommended ways to reduce gun violence. The National Rifle Association (NRA) responded on Twitter. The NRA supports gun ownership rights. It said, "Someone should tell self-important anti-gun doctors to stay in their lane." The NRA did not think doctors were gun control experts. Many doctors responded. Some tweeted selfies. The selfies showed doctors treating victims of gun violence. Doctors used the hashtag #ThisIsOurLane. These tweets showed the effects of gun violence.

National Rifle Association, Twitter Post, November 7, 2018, 11:43 am. www.twitter.com. status/1060256567914909702.

with certain mental illnesses are excluded.

So are **felons**. Courts have also ruled

that *arms* does not mean all weapons.

Students Demand Action activists march for better gun control laws. Students Demand Action is a nationwide campaign to end gun violence.

For example, courts have upheld bans on concealed weapons. These are hidden weapons. Laws also forbid guns in schools and government buildings.

On June 26, 2008, the US Supreme Court decided a case. The case was called *District of Columbia v. Heller.* Officials in Washington, DC, had banned handguns. The court's ruling overturned this ban. The court interpreted the Second Amendment. It said the amendment gives people the right to own and use guns for self-defense. This was the first time the Supreme Court had made such a ruling.

GUN OWNERSHIP

Many people want to increase the minimum gun ownership age. The minimum age to buy a handgun is twenty-one. A permit is also required in some states. The minimum age to buy a long gun is lower. Long guns are guns with long barrels. They include rifles and shotguns. Licensed dealers cannot sell long guns to people under eighteen. These are federal laws. Some states have their own laws. For example, the minimum age for long gun ownership is lower in Minnesota. Minnesotans can own a long gun at the age of fourteen. But they need to have a firearms safety certificate.

Some people buy guns from unlicensed sellers. These sellers can sell handguns to people who are eighteen or older. They can

Many people buy guns at gun shows.

sell long guns to people of any age. Some

unlicensed sellers sell guns at gun shows.

Licensed dealers must do background

checks. A background check shows

whether a potential buyer has a criminal

record. It may also show mental health

A woman protests the National Rifle Association at a 2018 rally in Florida.

issues. Certain mental health issues

may make it dangerous for someone

to own a gun. Dealers can sell guns to

people who pass background checks.

Unlicensed sellers do not have to do

background checks. They do not have to

ask for proof of age. This is called the gun show loophole.

Many people support stricter gun control laws. This includes background checks for all buyers. But not everyone agrees. Some people think stricter laws would not work. They worry that their Second Amendment rights would be restricted. Some people think the best solution is to give more people guns. They think this would allow more people to protect themselves.

Some people think better mental health reporting could help prevent gun violence. Background checks screen buyers for a history of mental illness. But states are not required to report mental health histories. Buyers with mental health issues may pass background checks. Other people think better school security is the answer.

SCHOOL SECURITY

Many schools are taking steps to prevent shootings. Some have installed metal detectors. Metal detectors sense metal objects. They can find hidden guns. Some schools give teachers panic buttons. Panic buttons are small devices. They are worn on clothing. Teachers can press these buttons during a shooting. This alerts police.

In the United States, many students learn lockdown or active shooter drills at a young age.

Many schools also have security cameras.

These cameras monitor the building.

Many schools have lockdown drills. Some also have active shooter drills. Active shooter drills prepare people for a shooting. A teacher or staff member may play the role of a shooter. The person may jiggle the handles of locked doors. Students practice

being silent.

Some schools have police officers

on campus. They are called resource

officers. Resource officers help keep the

THE FEDERAL COMMISSION ON SCHOOL SAFETY

The Federal Commission on School Safety was formed after the Parkland shooting. Its goal was to make schools safer. Education Secretary Betsy DeVos led the commission. It released a report in December 2018. The report recommends arming teachers. It said raising the minimum gun ownership age would not reduce school shootings. It does not suggest gun control. Many people disagree with the report.

school secure. They talk to students. They build relationships. Resource officers ensure students' safety.

In some schools, teachers keep bulletproof vests in classrooms. A few schools arm their teachers. For example, some South Dakota schools offer a training program. Teachers and staff can participate. Participants must attend eighty hours of training. They are taught how to use a gun. They also learn about first aid. Some schools in Arkansas, Utah, Idaho, and Texas have similar programs.

Many people have concerns about arming teachers. Some worry that students could get the weapons. Studies show that access to guns triples the risk of suicide. It also doubles the risk of murder. Some groups oppose arming teachers. This includes the National Education Association (NEA). The NEA is a group of teachers. It says lawmakers should keep guns away from schools. The National Association of School Resource Officers (NASRO) also opposes arming teachers. This group worries that police may mistake armed teachers for shooters. NASRO also worries

Some schools in Ohio have programs that arm teachers and show them how to use guns.

that teachers lack training. They may

not have enough training to keep guns

secure. It says this poses a risk to students

and teachers.

Experts say active shooter drills put

kids through **trauma**. Trauma is an

Students protest for better gun control laws at a march in California in 2018.

unpleasant experience. It causes emotional

problems. These drills may make students

feel like they are under attack. Students

may have a lot of stress and anxiety.

Some experts think armed teachers and metal detectors have the same effects.

Many people argue that drills and security measures do not address gun violence. They want more focus on gun control. They say making guns harder to buy is the best solution. Adam Lankford is a criminology professor. He works at the University of Alabama. He says, "Firearms availability is the primary reason why the United States has more public mass shooters than other countries."[5]

CHAPTER THREE

WHAT ARE RISK FACTORS FOR VIOLENCE?

Many risk factors contribute to gun violence. Gun violence can be linked to **poverty**. It is also connected to **discrimination**. In some cases, it is linked to mental health. People also need access to guns to become shooters. Researchers have discovered these links. Each of these

Many activists are trying to bring attention to gun violence in African American communities.

is a risk factor. Risk factors do not cause

violence. They simply make it more likely.

GUN VIOLENCE AND INEQUALITY

Most gun violence happens in poor

neighborhoods. These are usually

majority-black neighborhoods. Black people

experience higher rates of poverty than white people. They also experience higher rates of gun violence. This includes school shootings. Poor neighborhoods often have high rates of unemployment. Residents may not be able to get a good education. Schools may not have many resources. Residents have limited opportunities. These are all risk factors for violence.

Student Edna Chavez lives in South Los Angeles. This is a poor neighborhood in California. Chavez attended March for Our Lives in Washington, DC. This was a march against gun violence that occurred in 2018.

Los Angeles has a high rate of homelessness and poverty.

Chavez gave a speech at the march. She said, "It is normal to see flowers honoring the lives of black and brown youth that have lost their lives to a bullet."[6]

Mass shootings often get lots of news coverage. Not as much attention is paid to everyday gun violence. Dante Barry is a writer and an activist. He cofounded the Million Hoodies Movement for Justice. This group fights **racism** and violence. Barry said, "Communities that have been devastated by gun violence are still fighting for [recognition]."[7] He wants people to recognize that gun violence is a problem in black communities.

Most gun deaths in the United States are suicides. Poverty increases the risk of suicide. This risk also increases when people have access to guns. The weapon most often used in suicides in the United States is the handgun. Some of these

ACCESS TO FIREARMS

Most guns used in school shootings come from the shooter's home. The gun may belong to a parent or relative. About 42 percent of US adults have guns. Home gun safety could help reduce gun violence. Gun owners could store their guns securely. They could also store ammunition separately.

suicides happen in schools. Limiting access to guns could help reduce suicide and murder rates.

MASS SHOOTERS

Not much is known about the risk factors for mass shootings. The Federal Bureau of Investigation (FBI) profiles criminals.

It identifies features that make people likely to commit crimes. The FBI has not created a profile for mass shooters. It says creating one may be dangerous. Many people who will never become mass shooters may have similar features. They could be labeled as threats.

Still, mass shooters do have similarities. They are often bullied or ignored. They may feel alone. They may have low self-esteem. They may also worry about fitting in. Many shooters have recently experienced a loss. They may have been dumped by a partner.

Activists from the group Gays Against Guns hold photos of school shooting victims at a march in 2018.

They may feel upset or angry. These feelings can trigger violence.

Mass shooters often come from stable families. They live in middle- or upper-class neighborhoods. These neighborhoods often have low crime rates.

Some shooters have depression or other mental health illnesses. These illnesses often go untreated. Isolation and mental illness may make them feel lost. This may be one reason why they lash out.

MENTAL ILLNESS AND GENDER

Many people associate gun violence with mental illness. But mental illness does not predict gun violence. Most people who have mental illnesses are not violent. Jeffrey Swanson is a professor. He works at the Duke University School of Medicine.

HOW THE UNITED STATES STACKS UP

In 2018, CNN did a study. It reviewed school shootings in different countries. It looked at the years 2009 to 2018. The United States had the most school shootings. There were 288 US school shootings. Mexico ranked the second highest. There were eight school shootings in Mexico in that time. The United States has just 4.4 percent of the world's people. But Americans own 42 percent of the world's guns.

He says, "Even if we had a perfect mental health care system, that is not going to solve our gun violence problem."[8]

Most mass shooters are young white men. Researchers have some ideas about why this is the case. Men may be more

Many women and people of color are involved in the fight against gun violence.

prone to violence than women. This is

because of learned behaviors. Society

has different expectations for boys than

it does for girls. Boys are often taught to

be aggressive. Men also tend to have more

privileges than women. Privilege can make people feel like they are better than others.

Race plays a role too. White people often have more opportunities than people of color. White men may think they deserve certain privileges. They may lash out when something does not go their way. For example, this may happen if they are fired from a job. They may feel like they have been treated unfairly. They may become angry and violent.

CHAPTER FOUR

WHAT'S NEXT FOR GUN CONTROL?

Stricter gun control laws could help reduce school shootings. Some US states have red flag laws. These laws apply in cases where gun owners are likely to commit violence. Family members of the gun owners ask a judge for a court order. Police can also do this. This order requires

In 2018, some students organized walkouts to raise awareness of school shootings. Walkouts occur when students leave classrooms in protest.

people to give their guns to police. The order is temporary. Police can give the guns back when it is safe to do so. As of March 2019, fourteen states had red flag laws. Washington, DC, also has a red flag law.

GUN CONTROL LAWS

The US House of Representatives
passed the STOP School Violence Act
in March 2018. The act would give funds
for school security. It also offers funds for
special training. School officials would
receive this training. They would learn how
to deal with mental health crises. As of early
2019, the act was still a bill. It was being
considered in the US Senate. The president
reviews bills that pass through the Senate.
The president may sign them. Then they
become law.

Many states passed bills in 2019 to address gun violence. In some states, the minimum age to buy long guns was increased to twenty-one. In January 2019, the House introduced a gun control bill. It is called the Universal Background Checks bill. It would require almost all gun buyers

A NEW INVENTION

In 2018, a high school student made a metal device. It attaches to the base of a door. It creates a stronger barrier than a normal bolt lock. This device could help protect people during a school shooting. School districts in Wisconsin are now using this device.

Many people are in support of universal background checks.

to go through background checks. Law

enforcement officers would be exempt.

People buying guns from close family

members would also be exempt. The bill

could close the gun show loophole.

The House will likely vote on the bill

in 2019. The bill is not expected to pass

in the Senate. But activists are ready for

the challenge. Jaclyn Corin is a Parkland

student. Corin and other activists plan to

fight for the bill's passage.

ACTIVIST GROUPS

Activism is another way to fight gun

violence. Activists raise awareness of the

issue. They pressure lawmakers to change

laws. Many activists are shooting survivors.

Others are family members of shooting

victims. The group Moms Demand Action

was formed in 2012 after a school shooting. The shooting happened on December 14. A shooter entered Sandy Hook Elementary School. This school is in Newtown, Connecticut. The shooter killed twenty-six people. He also killed himself. Twenty of the victims were children. Moms Demand Action fought for tougher gun control laws. It raised awareness about school shootings. It merged with another activist group in 2013. The larger group is called Everytown for Gun Safety. This group gathers data about school shootings. It educates lawmakers about gun violence.

Some mothers whose families had been affected by gun violence joined Moms Demand Action.

On March 24, 2018, Parkland survivors

led a march. The march occurred in

Washington, DC. It was called March

for Our Lives. Hundreds of thousands of

people joined their cause. Similar marches happened across the United States. They also happened around the world.

Parkland survivors asked for better gun control laws. They asked for a ban on assault weapons. They wanted universal background checks. They confronted the NRA. Survivor and activist Emma Gonzalez gave a speech. She called for gun control reforms. She said, "If you actively do nothing, people continually end up dead."[9]

March for Our Lives is now a national organization. It has more than 200 chapters. It hopes to add more. The group raises

Jaclyn Corin and other Parkland survivors spoke at the March for Our Lives protest in Washington, DC.

awareness of gun violence. It also

encourages young people to vote. Voters

can elect lawmakers who are pro-gun

control. These lawmakers could help pass

stricter gun control laws.

Some gun rights groups also support gun control. Gun Owners for Responsible Ownership (GOFRO) is a group of gun enthusiasts. GOFRO works with public health professionals. It helps develop suicide prevention programs. It also supports universal background checks.

PREPARATION AND PREVENTION

School shootings make up a small part of overall gun violence. But they are a serious issue. Schools encourage students to speak up if they are aware of a threat.

Many schools prepare students for shootings. But preparation does not

SUICIDE AND SHOOTINGS

Shooting survivors may have PTSD. They may also have depression. Family members of victims may have these conditions too. These conditions can increase a person's risk for suicide. Two suicide deaths followed the Columbine shooting. A survivor died by suicide. So did the mother of a student who was injured in the shooting. In 2019, two Parkland survivors died by suicide. Another suicide victim was the father of a student killed at Sandy Hook.

address the problem. Stricter gun control laws may be the solution. Some politicians are trying to pass stricter gun control laws. These laws may help prevent and reduce shootings in the future.

GLOSSARY

amendment

a change or an addition to an existing law

bill

a written document that can become law if passed by the government

discrimination

the unjust treatment of a person or group based on race or other perceived differences

felon

a criminal who has committed a serious crime, such as murder

poverty

the condition of being poor

racism

the belief that certain people are better than others because of their race

suicide

the act of purposefully killing oneself as a result of mental illness

trauma

a mix of strong and negative emotions that result from an unpleasant and frightening experience

SOURCE NOTES

CHAPTER ONE: WHAT IS THE HISTORY OF SCHOOL SHOOTINGS?

1. Quoted in Martin Kaste, "Despite Heightened Fear of School Shootings, It's Not a Growing Epidemic," *NPR*, March 15, 2018. www.npr.org.

2. Quoted in Martin Kaste, "Despite Heightened Fear of School Shootings, It's Not a Growing Epidemic."

CHAPTER TWO: HOW ARE PEOPLE ADDRESSING SCHOOL SHOOTINGS?

3. Quoted in "Senators Introduce Assault Weapons Ban," *United States Senator for California Dianne Feinstein*, January 9, 2019. www.feinstein.senate.gov.

4. Quoted in "Second Amendment," *Legal Information Institute*, n.d. www.law.cornell.edu.

5. Quoted in Miriam Valverde, "Did Mass Shootings Increase 200 Percent Since Assault Weapons Ban Expired?" *PolitiFact*, February 23, 2018. www.politifact.com.

CHAPTER THREE: WHAT ARE RISK FACTORS FOR VIOLENCE?

6. Quoted in Samantha Raphelson and Emma Bowman, "Hundreds of Thousands March for Gun Control Across the U.S." *NPR*, March 24, 2018. www.npr.org.

7. Quoted in Sarah Ruiz-Grossman, "We Need to Talk About Black Lives and Gun Violence After the Florida Shooting," *HuffPost*, February 22, 2018. www.huffingtonpost.com.

8. Quoted in Lois Beckett, "Myth vs. Fact: Violence and Mental Health," *ProPublica*, June 10, 2014. www.propublica.org.

CHAPTER FOUR: WHAT'S NEXT FOR GUN CONTROL?

9. Quoted in "Politics in the News: Gun-Violence Restraining Order," *NPR*, February 19, 2018. www.npr.org.

FOR FURTHER RESEARCH

BOOKS

Eric Braun, *Never Again: The Parkland Shooting and the Teen Activists Leading a Movement*. Minneapolis, MN: Lerner Publications, 2019.

Tamra Orr, *Tucson Shooting and Gun Control*. Ann Arbor, MI: Cherry Lake Publishing, 2018.

INTERNET SOURCES

Editorial Staff of *The Eagle Eye, Guardian*, "Our Manifesto to Fix America's Gun Laws," March 23, 2018. www.theguardian.com.

Christine Hauser, "What to Do When There's an Active Shooter," *New York Times*, February 16, 2018. www.nytimes.com.

Richard Pérez-Peña, "Gun Control Explained," *New York Times*, October 7, 2015. www.nytimes.com.

Linda Qiu and Justin Bank, "Checking Facts and Falsehoods about Mental Illness After Parkland Shooting," *New York Times*, February 16, 2018. www.nytimes.com.

WEBSITES

The Gun Violence Archive
www.gunviolencearchive.org

The Gun Violence Archive provides data and information about gun violence in the United States.

March For Our Lives
www.marchforourlives.com

March For Our Lives is a student-led activist organization. Its goal is to reduce gun violence in the United States.

Ready.Gov
www.ready.gov

Ready.Gov gives information on how people can respond and protect themselves during a shooting.

INDEX

IMAGE CREDITS

ABOUT THE AUTHOR

Jen Barton is an award-winning author of many books for kids. When she's not reading or writing, you can probably find her baking or out for a hike. Just a short girl with a tall imagination, Jen lives in California with her husband and their peculiar little dog.